PALM BEACH COUNTY
LIBRARY SYSTEM
3650 Summit Boulevard
West Palm Beach, FL 33406-4198

bake me I'm yours...

whoopie pies

Jill Collins &
Natalie Saville

D&C
David and Charles
www.rucraft.co.uk

A DAVID & CHARLES BOOK

© F&W Media International, LTD 2011

David & Charles is an imprint of
F&W Media International, LTD
Brunel House, Forde Close, Newton Abbot,
TQ12 4PU, UK

F&W Media International, LTD is a subsidiary
of F+W Media, Inc.
4700 East Galbraith Road, Cincinnati,
OH 45236

First published in the UK & US in 2011

Text and designs copyright © Jill Collins and
Natalie Saville 2011
Photography and illustrations © F&W Media
International LTD 2011

Jill Collins and Natalie Saville have asserted
their right to be identified as authors of this work
in accordance with the Copyright, Designs and
Patents Act, 1988.

dedication

To our ever-supportive husbands,
Jeremy and Andy, and to our
gorgeous children, Ashley, Elena,
Joe and Jake, who have been
incredibly enthusiastic throughout,
and have loved every design we
have ever come up with.

Names of manufacturers, products and product
ranges are provided for the information of
readers, with no intention to infringe copyright
or trademarks.

A catalogue record for this book is available from
the British Library.

ISBN-13: 978-1-4463-0068-8 hardback
ISBN-10: 1-4463-0068-4 hardback

Printed in China by RR Donnelley
for F&W Media International, LTD
Brunel House, Forde Close, Newton Abbot,
TQ12 4PU, UK

10 9 8 7 6 5 4 3 2 1

Publisher Alison Myer
Editor James Brooks
Project Editor Ame Verso
Senior Designer Victoria Marks
Photography Sian Irvine and Joe Giacomet
Production Manager Bev Richardson

F+W Media publishes high quality books on a
wide range of subjects. For more great book ideas
visit: www.rucraft.co.uk

Contents

whoopie!

Whoopie pies are the latest craze to hit big stores and bijoux bakeries everywhere – little mounds of cakey goodness, sandwiched together with delicious, gooey fillings. While they have been around in the USA for a long time, the rest of the world is finally starting to catch on. Originating in Pennsylvania, folklore has it that Amish women would bake them as a dessert for their husbands' and children's lunchboxes and when they found these special treats they would shout 'whoopie!'

Traditionally, whoopies are chocolate flavoured with a marshmallow cream filling, but the basic recipe can be easily adapted for a wide variety of other flavours and fillings by adding or changing a few ingredients.

When we were first asked to write a book about whoopie pies, we immediately scoured the internet for information and selflessly visited many major stores to buy and try them (Natalie even flew to New York in search of whoopies!). What struck us most profoundly was that all whoopies looked the same. Granted, they were baked in a variety of different flavours, but other than the odd dusting of sprinkles, or dab of fondant icing, none of them were decorated in any way. With our background in cake design and decoration, we felt that here was an opportunity to transfer our skills with cakes and cupcakes onto whoopie pies – and this book is the result.

As you will see from the creations that follow, whoopie pies don't need to be the cupcake's poor relation – they can shine every bit as much, and sometimes more so, as the domed shape of the whoopie lends itself beautifully to some projects, much more so than the flat iced cupcake.

We hope you have as much fun trying out the designs in this book as we did dreaming them up. Each project has a difficulty rating shown in little whoopies – start with the easy ones and move on to the more complex designs as your confidence grows. Happy decorating!

Jill and Natalie

www.thegreatlittlecakecompany.co.uk

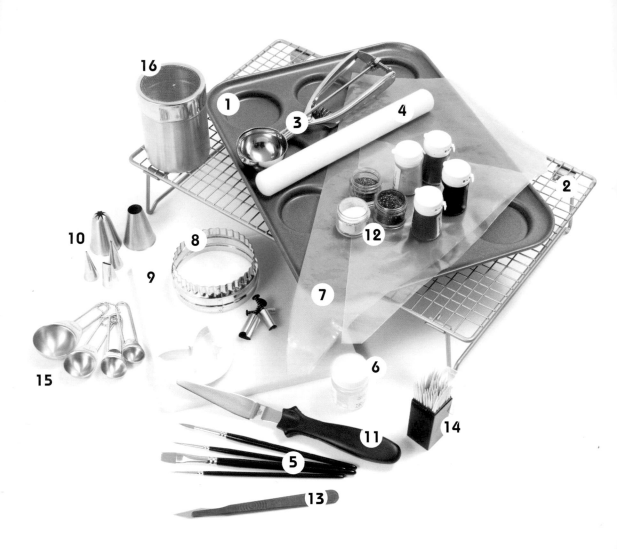

tools and equipment

To make a batch of whoopie pies, you don't need much more than you'll find in any domestic kitchen, but if you are planning on trying your hand at decorating, here is a list of the key tools and equipment you might find helpful:

1. Whoopie pie tin – very useful, but greased baking trays can be used instead
2. Wire rack – for placing whoopies on to cool
3. Small ice cream scoop – for measuring batter for perfect-sized whoopies every time
4. Non-stick rolling pin – for rolling out sugarpaste and petal paste
5. Paintbrushes – a variety of different sizes are useful for painting, moistening and sticking
6. Edible glue – for sticking small pieces of icing together
7. Piping (pastry) bags – small for piping royal icing and large for filling whoopies
8. Cutters – a variety of cutters are useful for different projects
9. Drying mat – a great place to dry small sugarpaste pieces
10. Piping tubes (tips) – for filling, piping and decoration (also known as nozzles)
11. Palette knife – for lifting delicate sugarpaste pieces
12. Paste food colours, edible dusts and edible glitters – for colouring, painting and adding sparkle
13. Craft knife – for accurate detailed cutting
14. Cocktail sticks (toothpicks) – great for adding tiny amounts of colour and for frilling
15. Measuring spoons – for measuring ingredients quickly and accurately
16. Sugar shaker – for dusting your surface with icing (confectioners') sugar to prevent sticking

whoopie recipes

A great whoopie pie should be moist, dense and slightly sticky – the perfect hybrid of cake and cookie, with a generous mouthful of filling in every bite. All of the recipes in this book will make 12 whoopies or 40 mini whoopies.

the perfect whoopie...

Making whoopie pies is not difficult but there are a few points to bear in mind to guarantee greatness...

- Always use the best and freshest ingredients you can.
- Always bring your ingredients to room temperature before you start baking, to avoid curdling.
- Always preheat your oven.
- Make sure your whoopies are just firm to the touch before removing from the oven or they tend to sink after a few minutes.
- Allow whoopies to cool completely before filling and decorating.
- Whoopies can be baked in any colour you like by adding some food colouring to the batter (see Techniques).

- If you don't have whoopie pie tins, you can use baking sheets lined with greaseproof paper. Drop scoops of batter at evenly spaced intervals, but not too close together as the mixture tends to spread.
- To make mini whoopies, follow your chosen whoopie recipe, but use mini muffin tins and 10ml (2 level tsp) batter in each well. Bake for approximately ten minutes or until they are just firm to the touch.
- Whoopie pies are best eaten fresh but can be stored in an airtight container for up to three days. They can also be frozen for up to a month. For best results, freeze in single layers – once frozen they can be stacked on top of each other in a sealed container for easy storage.

chocolate whoopie

The original and quintessential whoopie pie.

ingredients...

- 115g (4oz) soft unsalted (sweet) butter
- 200g (7oz) soft brown sugar
- 1 large (US extra large) egg
- 5ml (1 tsp) vanilla extract
- 225ml (8 fl oz) buttermilk
- 60g (2oz) cocoa powder (unsweetened cocoa)
- 5ml (1 tsp) bicarbonate of soda
- 2.5ml (½ tsp) baking powder
- 190g (6¾oz) plain (all-purpose) flour

1 Preheat the oven to 180°C (350°F/Gas 4). Grease two whoopie pie tins with a little softened butter.

2 Sift together the flour, cocoa, baking powder and bicarbonate of soda and set aside.

3 In a separate bowl, cream the butter and sugar together until light and fluffy using an electric whisk or freestanding mixer.

4 Add the egg and vanilla and beat until well combined.

5 Fold in half the flour mixture, followed by half the buttermilk. Repeat with remaining ingredients.

6 Drop 1½ tbsp or a level small ice cream scoopful of batter into each well of the tins.

7 Bake for approximately 12 minutes or until the whoopies feel just firm to the touch. Allow to cool in the tins for five minutes before transferring to a wire rack to cool completely.

double trouble...
Add a good handful of chocolate chips to the batter for a decadent double chocolate treat!

vanilla whoopie

A fantastically versatile whoopie – the perfect canvas for the most daring of fillings!

ingredients...

- 115g (4oz) soft unsalted (sweet) butter
- 200g (7oz) caster (superfine) sugar
- 1 large (US extra large) egg
- 7.5ml (1½ tsp) vanilla extract
- 225ml (8 fl oz) buttermilk
- 5ml (1 tsp) bicarbonate of soda
- 2.5ml (½ tsp) baking powder
- 275g (9¾oz) plain (all-purpose) flour

1 Preheat the oven to 180°C (350°F/Gas 4). Grease two whoopie pie tins with a little softened butter.

2 Sift together the flour, baking powder and bicarbonate of soda and set aside.

3 In a separate bowl, cream the butter and sugar together until light and fluffy using an electric whisk or freestanding mixer.

4 Add the egg and vanilla and beat until well combined.

5 Fold in half the flour mixture, followed by half the buttermilk. Repeat with remaining ingredients.

6 Drop 1½ tbsp or a level small ice cream scoopful of batter into each well of the tins.

7 Bake for approximately 12 minutes or until the whoopies feel just firm to the touch. Allow to cool in the tins for five minutes before transferring to a wire rack to cool completely.

flavour boost...
For a more intense flavour and an authentic look, replace the vanilla extract with seeds scraped from a vanilla pod.

red velvet whoopie

Another firm favourite among whoopie aficionados.

ingredients...

- 115g (4oz) soft unsalted (sweet) butter
- 200g (7oz) caster (superfine) sugar
- 1 large (US extra large) egg
- 5ml (1 tsp) vanilla extract
- 5ml (1 tsp) white vinegar
- 30g (1oz) cocoa powder (unsweetened cocoa)
- 225ml (8 fl oz) buttermilk
- 5ml (1 tsp) bicarbonate of soda
- 240g (8½oz) plain (all-purpose) flour
- 2.5ml (½ tsp) red paste food colour

1 Preheat the oven to 180°C (350°F/Gas 4). Grease two whoopie pie tins with a little softened butter.

2 Sift together the flour and bicarbonate of soda and set aside.

3 In a separate bowl, cream the butter and sugar together until light and fluffy using an electric whisk or freestanding mixer.

4 Add the egg and beat until well combined.

5 In a small bowl, mix the cocoa, vanilla, vinegar and red paste food colour until you have a smooth paste, then mix in to the batter.

6 Fold in half the flour mixture, followed by half the buttermilk. Repeat with remaining ingredients.

7 Drop 1½ tbsp or a level small ice cream scoopful of batter into each well of the tins.

8 Bake for approximately 12 minutes or until the whoopies feel just firm to the touch. Allow to cool in the tins for five minutes before transferring to a wire rack to cool completely.

red or dead...
Don't be afraid to add lots of colour – a red velvet whoopie can never be too red!

apple pie whoopie

A truly irresistible combination of apples and spices make this whoopie an all-time family favourite.

ingredients...

- 115g (4oz) soft unsalted (sweet) butter
- 200g (7oz) soft brown sugar
- 1 large (US extra large) egg
- 2.5ml (½ tsp) vanilla extract
- 225g (8oz) apple sauce
- 5ml (1 tsp) baking powder
- 5ml (1 tsp) cinnamon
- 1.25ml (¼ tsp) ground cloves
- 190g (6¾oz) plain (all-purpose) flour

1 Preheat the oven to 180°C (350°f/Gas 4). Grease two whoopie pie tins with a little softened butter.
2 Sift together the flour, cinnamon, cloves and bicarbonate of soda and set aside.
3 In a separate bowl, cream the butter and sugar together until light and fluffy using an electric whisk or freestanding mixer.
4 Add the egg and vanilla and beat until well combined.
5 Fold in half the flour mixture, followed by half the apple sauce. Repeat with remaining ingredients.
6 Drop 1½ tbsp or a level small ice cream scoopful of batter into each well of the tins.
7 Bake for approximately 12–14 minutes or until the whoopies feel just firm to the touch. Allow to cool in the tins for five minutes before transferring to a wire rack to cool completely.

hot to trot...
These whoopies are best eaten warm
– nobody can resist them long enough
to let them cool down anyway!

banana whoopie

A marvellously moist teatime treat.

ingredients...

- 115g (4oz) soft unsalted (sweet) butter
- 200g (7oz) soft brown sugar
- 1 large (US extra large) egg
- 5ml (1 tsp) vanilla extract
- 225g (8oz) very ripe mashed banana
- 5ml (1 tsp) bicarbonate of soda
- 2.5ml (½ tsp) baking powder
- 2.5ml (½ tsp) cinnamon
- 250g (8¾oz) plain (all-purpose) flour

1 Preheat the oven to 180°C (350°F/Gas 4). Grease two whoopie pie tins with a little softened butter.
2 Sift together the flour, cinnamon, baking powder and bicarbonate of soda and set aside.
3 In a separate bowl, cream the butter and sugar together until light and fluffy using an electric whisk or freestanding mixer.
4 Add the egg and vanilla and beat until well combined.
5 Fold in half the flour mixture, followed by half the mashed banana. Repeat with remaining ingredients.
6 Drop 1½ tbsp or a level small ice cream scoopful of batter into each well of the tins.
7 Bake for approximately 12 minutes or until the whoopies feel just firm to the touch. Allow to cool in the tins for five minutes before transferring to a wire rack to cool completely.

go bananas...
These whoopies are a great way to use up any old bananas – the riper the better.

coconut whoopie

This whoopie is as close as you can get to a tropical paradise – all that's missing is the sunshine!

ingredients...

- 115g (4oz) soft unsalted (sweet) butter
- 200g (7oz) caster (superfine) sugar
- 1 large (US extra large) egg
- 225ml (8 fl oz) buttermilk
- 5ml (1 tsp) bicarbonate of soda
- 60ml (4 tbsp) desiccated (dry unsweetened shredded) coconut
- 250g (8¾oz) plain (all-purpose) flour

1 Preheat the oven to 180°C (350°F/Gas 4). Grease two whoopie pie tins with a little softened butter.
2 Sift together the flour and bicarbonate of soda. Add the coconut and set aside.
3 In a separate bowl, cream the butter and sugar together until light and fluffy using an electric whisk or freestanding mixer.
4 Add the egg and beat until well combined.
5 Fold in half the flour mixture, followed by half the buttermilk. Repeat with remaining ingredients.
6 Drop 1½ tbsp or a level small ice cream scoopful of batter into each well of the tins.
7 Bake for approximately 12 minutes or until the whoopies feel just firm to the touch. Allow to cool in the tins for five minutes before transferring to a wire rack to cool completely.

paradise punch...
For a more intense coconut flavour, add 1.25ml (¼ tsp) coconut essence – but beware – a little goes a long way!

fillings and toppings

When it comes to filling whoopies, the most traditional and widely known is the chocolate whoopie, filled with marshmallow cream filling. While this is a sublime combination, there are many variations that are equally delicious. Here we have included a few of our favourite recipes and combinations – mix and match at will! All of these recipes will fill 12 whoopies or 40 mini whoopies.

filling whoopies

Generously spread your chosen filling with a palette knife onto one half of the whoopie before placing the other half on top. For a neater look, snip off the end of a large, strong piping (pastry) bag at an angle, approximately 1cm (⅜in) up from the tip. Insert a large star or round tube (tip), spoon in the filling and twist the bag closed. Pipe the filling onto one whoopie half and position the other half on top.

vanilla buttercream filling

While this is a tasty filling in its own right, vanilla buttercream can easily be adapted to make a wide variety of other fantastic fillings – see box below.

ingredients...

- 200g (7oz) soft unsalted (sweet) butter
- 400g (14oz) sifted icing (confectioners') sugar
- 5ml (1 tsp) vanilla extract
- 15ml (1 tbsp) milk

1 Beat the butter with an electric whisk or freestanding mixer until light and fluffy.

2 Slowly beat in the sifted icing (confectioners') sugar and vanilla, adding milk as needed, until well incorporated.

flavour variations

- **Chocolate:** Substitute 80g (2¾oz) icing (confectioners') sugar with 80g (2¾oz) cocoa powder.
- **Lemon:** Add 150g (5¼oz) lemon curd to the vanilla buttercream and stir. Add more if you like it really tangy!
- **Victoria sponge:** Add a layer of raspberry or strawberry jam to the whoopie before piping the vanilla buttercream.
- **Peppermint:** Substitute 5ml (1 tsp) vanilla extract with 5ml (1 tsp) peppermint essence and add a dot or two of green paste food colour to make beautiful minty buttercream. Add a few chocolate chips and you have mint choc chip!

marshmallow cream filling

The original and arguably the best whoopie pie filling, marshmallow cream has to be tasted to be believed!

delicious in...
a red velvet whoopie

ingredients...

- 120g (4¼oz) soft unsalted (sweet) butter
- 220g (7¾oz) sifted icing (confectioners') sugar
- 5ml (1 tsp) vanilla extract
- 250g (8¾oz) marshmallow fluff (available from some supermarkets and online)

1 Beat the butter with an electric whisk or freestanding mixer until light and fluffy.

2 Slowly beat in the sifted icing (confectioners') sugar and vanilla until well incorporated.

3 Fold in the marshmallow fluff and stir gently until you have a smooth, creamy mixture.

cinnamon cream cheese filling

A classy combination of sweet, savoury and spicy, this filling works well with most whoopie flavours.

delicious in...
an apple pie whoopie

ingredients...

- 150g (5¼oz) cream cheese
- 30g (1oz) soft unsalted (sweet) butter
- 450g (1lb) sifted icing (confectioners') sugar
- 2.5ml (½ tsp) vanilla extract
- 2.5ml (½ tsp) cinnamon

1 Beat the butter and cream cheese together with an electric whisk or freestanding mixer until light and fluffy.

2 Slowly beat in the sifted icing (confectioners') sugar, cinnamon and vanilla until well incorporated.

coconut and lime filling

The perfect Caribbean combination!

delicious in...
a coconut whoopie

ingredients...

• 65g (2¼oz) desiccated (dry unsweetened shredded) coconut

• 220g (7¾oz) soft unsalted (sweet) butter

• 400g (14oz) sifted icing (confectioners') sugar

• Juice of one lime

1 Toast the coconut in a dry frying pan for a couple of minutes (or until light brown and fragrant), stirring constantly, then leave to cool completely.

2 Beat the butter with an electric whisk or freestanding mixer until light and fluffy.

3 Slowly beat in the sifted icing (confectioners') sugar and lime juice until well incorporated.

4 Stir in the toasted coconut.

creamy maple syrup filling

Mmmm ... seriously smooth and moreish – definitely one of our favourites!

delicious in...
a banana whoopie

ingredients...

• 80g (2¾oz) soft unsalted (sweet) butter

• 400g (14oz) sifted icing (confectioners') sugar

• 80ml (2¾ fl oz) double cream

• 120ml (4¼ fl oz) maple syrup

1 Beat the butter with an electric whisk or freestanding mixer until light and fluffy.

2 Slowly beat in the sifted icing (confectioners') sugar and maple syrup.

3 Add the cream and whisk on a very low speed, or by hand, to incorporate.

peanut butter cream filling

People go nuts for this divine filling.

delicious in...
a chocolate whoopie

ingredients...

- 150g (5¼oz) soft unsalted (sweet) butter
- 300g (10½oz) smooth or crunchy peanut butter
- 150g (5¼oz) sifted icing (confectioners') sugar
- 2.5ml (½ tsp) vanilla extract
- 15ml (1 tbsp) milk

1 Beat the butter and peanut butter together with an electric whisk or freestanding mixer until light and fluffy.
2 Slowly beat in the sifted icing (confectioners') sugar and vanilla, adding milk as needed, until well incorporated.

chocolate ganache topping

delicious in...
a vanilla whoopie

This decadent chocolate topping is best made the night before and allowed to cool and thicken naturally. However, the process can be speeded up by placing the bowl in the fridge for a few hours.

ingredients...

- 300ml (10 fl oz) double cream
- 150g (5¼oz) milk chocolate
- 150g (5¼oz) plain (semisweet) chocolate (minimum 50 percent cocoa solids)

1 Pour the cream into a saucepan and gently bring it to the boil, stirring to prevent burning. Break the chocolate into squares and put in a large bowl.
2 Once the cream comes to the boil, take off the heat and pour over the chocolate, stirring until all the chocolate has melted. Set aside to cool and thicken. Spread thickly on top of your whoopies.

sugarpaste

This is widely available in major supermarkets and online. Sugarpaste (rolled fondant) is easy to roll and colour (see Techniques), and is perfect as a base for many designs. A large number of whoopies in this book begin with a circle of sugarpaste fixed to the top.

petal paste

Also known as flower paste, this is similar to sugarpaste but hardens quicker and can be rolled out much more thinly without breaking. It dries to a hard, china-like finish and is perfect for making more delicate items such as cut-out numbers, flowers and butterflies. Petal paste is available in white and in many different colours from specialist sugarcraft shops and online.

royal icing

Royal icing is widely used for piping and sticking. It is readily available as a packet mix from many supermarkets but can be very easily made at home. This recipe makes approximately 250g (4–5 heaped tbsp), which can then be coloured as desired (see Techniques).

ingredients...
- 1 large (US extra large) egg white
- 250g (8¾oz) sifted icing (confectioners') sugar

1 Whisk the egg white in a large, clean bowl until foamy using an electric whisk.
2 Gradually beat in the icing (confectioners') sugar and continue beating until the icing is bright white and glossy (approximately two minutes). Finish beating with a wooden spoon. If needed, add drops of water sparingly to thin the icing, or a small amount of sifted icing (confectioners') sugar to stiffen it.
3 Once made, transfer to an airtight plastic container, lay some cling film (plastic wrap) directly on top of the icing, seal and store in the fridge. It will keep for two to three weeks like this. Beat briefly with a wooden spoon before use.

techniques

rolling out sugarpaste and petal paste

Remove all jewellery before rolling to avoid marking the paste. Lightly dust a clean work surface with icing (confectioners') sugar then knead the sugarpaste until soft and pliable, adding more icing (confectioners') sugar if it becomes too sticky. Mould into a ball and then roll out using a plastic non-stick rolling pin, turning regularly, and re-dusting the work surface to avoid sticking. For best results with petal paste, roll out on a white plastic board.

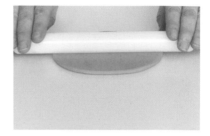

cutting out shapes

For hand cutting, use a very sharp craft knife to avoid wrinkling the sugarpaste or petal paste. When using cutters, position the cutter on top of the paste and press down firmly. For simple shapes, twist the cutter to ensure a clean edge. For complex shapes such as numbers, roll out a small amount of paste on the work surface, turn the cutter upside down, transfer the paste and re-roll it directly onto the cutter. Smooth the sides with a finger to give a clean edge. Remove the cut shape by tapping or pushing gently in the centre with the end of a paintbrush. Place on a foam mat to dry. For perfect cut outs from petal paste, it needs to be rolled out as thinly as possible – until it is almost transparent.

frilling

Place the piece of paste to be frilled on a foam mat. Take a cocktail stick (toothpick) in your right hand and place the other end across the paste. Using the index finger of your left hand, roll the cocktail stick (toothpick) back and forth across the paste until it frills. Continue all round the shape in this fashion until all edges are beautifully frilled.

shaping flowers

Flowers can be shaped in two main ways: firstly, by pressing a ball tool into the centre to cup the flower (this works best on small flowers); and secondly, by placing them into a small cup shape (e.g. the well of a paint palette) as soon as they have been made. Once dry the flower will hold its shape. For small flowers, sugarpaste works well. For larger flowers, use thinly rolled petal paste, which hardens to a china-like consistency.

piping

Snip off the end of a piping (pastry) bag at an angle, approximately 1cm (⅜in) up from the tip. Slip in the tube (tip) then spoon in the royal icing. Twist the bag to force the icing towards the tip. Hold the bag firmly in one hand with your thumb over the top and fingers either side and steady it with your other hand. Squeeze gently, holding the tube (tip) about 2–3cm (¾–1in) above the line you wish to pipe.

piping leaves

Follow the same procedure as described on the previous page, only insert a leaf tube (tip) (no. 51) into the piping (pastry) bag. Hold the bag with the open 'V' of the tube (tip) to the side, and then squeeze and jiggle the bag, reducing the pressure as you pull back, ending in a point.

piping hair

The tube (tip) used for hair depends on the type of hair you are trying to pipe: curly or straight. A basketweave tube (tip) (no. 47) is ideal, as it has one straight side and one zigzag side, so can be used for either type of hair depending on which way you hold the tube (tip). Start in the centre (or to one side if you want a side parting) and apply even pressure to the bag, holding it away from the head and allowing it to fall gently down. For short spiky hair, press down gently to release a small blob of icing, and then pull up sharply. Alternatively, apply icing with the flat side of a palette knife. Final adjustments can be made with a cocktail stick (toothpick).

painting faces

You will need white, blue and/or brown and black edible dusts, rejuvenator spirit for mixing and a very fine paintbrush (0000 is ideal). Start by painting the whites of the eyes, then add the iris colour, then the pupil, then a white highlight and finally the eyelashes, making sure you wash the brush between colours and you let each stage dry before adding the next. A cotton bud (cotton swab) dipped in clear alcohol is useful to remove mistakes.

using wires

Wires must never be inserted directly into a cake. Instead, push a plastic posy pick into the top and anchor the wires inside using a small ball of sugarpaste. To display numbers, letters or shapes on wires, make twice as many shapes as needed and attach back to back, sandwiching the wires in between with edible glue.

making figures

CMC (Tylo) powder gives extra strength to sugarpaste. Once made, use immediately or store in double-wrapped cling film (plastic wrap) until needed. Use a stick of dry spaghetti inserted into the body of your figure to support and reinforce the head, but remember to remove this before eating!

colouring

Colour can be added to all whoopies, icings and fillings. A little colour goes a long way, so always use a tiny amount on the end of a cocktail stick (toothpick) to add colour gradually, stirring or kneading well between each addition. It is much easier to add colour than to take it away, so be careful! Paste food colours (available from sugarcraft stores and online) are much better to use than liquid colours, as you need much less to make the colours vibrant. If you do use liquid colours, add slightly less of one of the other liquid ingredients to compensate so that the batter or icing does not become too runny.

masterpiece sunflowers

You don't need to be Van Gogh to be proud of these sunflower whoopies — and your artistry will be appreciated by all who see them.

you will need...

- five yellow whoopies filled with yellow buttercream
- sugarpaste: 250g (8¾oz) white
- petal paste: 40g (1½oz) yellow
- cutters: 10cm (4in) circle, large sunflower
- paint palette or ten shallow dishes
- 30ml (2 tbsp) brown royal icing in a piping (pastry) bag with no. 2 tube (tip)

1 Roll out the petal paste very thinly and cut ten sunflowers. Place each one in a small shallow dish or paint palette to dry in a cupped shape. Leave to dry overnight.

2 Roll out the white sugarpaste to around 2mm (¹⁄₁₆in) thick and cut five 10cm (4in) circles. Moisten the undersides with a damp paintbrush and fix on top of the whoopies, smoothing down the sides.

3 Fix one sunflower on top of each whoopie with a dot of royal icing. Pipe another dot of royal icing in the centre of each flower and place the second flower on top, slightly offset. Fill the centres by piping brown dots in concentric circles.

make it different...
Turn the sunflowers into daisies or gerberas by making them in white or in lots of bright colours.

Recipes whoopies, buttercream, royal icing   *Techniques* colouring, shaping flowers, piping

butterfly kisses

These butterflies with their delicate wings and just a touch of sparkle are so pretty they are sure to be a hit with girls of any age.

you will need...

- six filled vanilla whoopies

- sugarpaste: 300g (10½oz) white

- petal paste: 15g (½oz) each white, pink, green

- cutters: 10cm (4in) circle, butterfly

- card

- royal icing in piping (pastry) bags with no. 2 tubes (tips): 15ml (1 tbsp) each pink, pale green

- white edible glitter

1 Roll out the petal pastes very thinly and cut two butterflies from each colour. Dry each butterfly by resting it over a folded piece of card for a couple of hours or overnight.

2 When dry, brush the white butterflies with a damp paintbrush and sprinkle with white edible glitter. Pipe pink dots on the green butterflies and pipe green dots on the pink butterflies.

3 Roll out the white sugarpaste to around 2mm (¹⁄₁₆in) thick and cut six 10cm (4in) circles. Moisten the undersides with a damp paintbrush and fix on top of the whoopies, smoothing down the sides.

4 Pipe a thin line of royal icing on the underside of each butterfly and fix one in the centre of each whoopie. Pipe a body down the centre of each butterfly and sprinkle all over with white edible glitter.

make it special...
Decorate the butterflies with multicoloured edible glitters to make a dazzling kaleidoscope of colour.

Recipes   vanilla whoopies, fillings, royal icing   *Techniques*   cutting out shapes, piping

daisy chain

Nothing epitomizes lazy summer days more than a daisy chain. This simple design is perfect to eat while relaxing on the lawn!

you will need...

- filled whoopie (flavour of your choice)
- sugarpaste: 50g (1¾oz) white
- petal paste: 5g (⅛oz) white
- cutters: 10cm (4in) circle, small daisy
- foam pad and ball tool
- royal icing in piping (pastry) bags with no. 2 tubes (tips): 15ml (1 tbsp) each green, yellow

1 Roll out the petal paste very thinly and cut six daisies. Place the daisies on the foam pad and press gently in the centre with the ball tool to cup the petals. Leave to dry for a couple of hours or overnight.

2 Roll out the white sugarpaste to around 2mm (⅟₁₆in) thick and cut a 10cm (4in) circle. Moisten the underside with a damp paintbrush and fix on top of the whoopie, smoothing down the sides.

3 Secure the daisies around the edge of the whoopie with a dab of royal icing. Pipe a green line between each daisy to make the chain and pipe a yellow dot in the centre of each daisy.

accidents happen...
It's a good idea to make a few extra daisies as they are very delicate and break easily.

Recipes whoopies, fillings, royal icing   *Techniques* rolling out sugarpaste, shaping flowers, piping

rosebud romance

These beautiful whoopies are so romantic and stylish – and very easy to make. The instructions are for the red version, but you can make them in any shade.

you will need...

- filled whoopie pie (flavour of your choice)
- sugarpaste: 50g (1¾oz) white, 20g (¾oz) deep red
- 10cm (4in) circle cutter
- 15ml (1 tbsp) pale green royal icing in a piping (pastry) bag with no. 57 leaf tube (tip)
- white edible glitter

1 Roll out the red sugarpaste very thinly and cut three strips, each measuring 1 x 4cm (⅜ x 1½in). Gently flatten one long side of each strip with a rolling pin to thin it slightly.

2 With the flattened edge uppermost, roll up each strip to form a little rosebud. Allow to dry for a couple of hours or overnight.

3 Roll out the white sugarpaste to around 2mm (¹⁄₁₆in) thick and cut a 10cm (4in) circle. Moisten the underside with a damp paintbrush and fix on top of the whoopie, smoothing down the sides. Fix the rosebuds in the centre with a dab of royal icing.

4 To finish, pipe a small leaf between each rosebud with green royal icing then sprinkle the whoopie with a little white edible glitter.

pipe dreams...
If you don't have a no. 57 leaf tube (tip), cut a small inverted 'V' into the end of a piping (pastry) bag and use this instead.

Recipes whoopies, fillings, royal icing *Techniques* rolling out sugarpaste, piping leaves

flower power

Whoopie pies can be made to look gorgeous so simply by using different sized and shaped flower cutters.

divine daisy

Use a large daisy cutter and dry in a small shallow dish. Pipe the centre to match your colour scheme.

wild rose

Cut two flowers using a rose cutter. Thin the petals using a ball tool and dry in a shallow dish. Stick one on top of the other and fill the centre with coloured sugar.

bijoux blossoms

Make lots of tiny flowers using a blossom plunger cutter for a pretty, lacy effect.

pink and prickly

Carpet the top of a whoopie with a multitude of spiky pink flowers – and don't forget to pipe the centres!

pretty in pink

These rounded blossoms are so lovely – they look gorgeous in different shades of pink.

rose in bloom

This beautiful rose will look spectacular at any gathering – just imagine a whole bouquet of them!

you will need...

- filled vanilla whoopie
- sugarpaste: 50g (1¾oz) white, 5g (⅛oz) pale green
- petal paste: 8g (¼oz) pale pink
- cutters: 10cm (4in) circle, medium rose, medium leaf
- foam pad and ball tool
- kitchen foil
- white edible glitter
- edible glue

for the rose

1 Mould 2g (¹⁄₁₆oz) petal paste into a cone shape and set aside to dry. Roll out the remainder very thinly and cut one set of rose petals.

2 Place the petals on a foam pad and thin and frill the edges with a ball tool. Moisten the centre of the shape and all but the top quarter of each petal.

3 Place the cone in the centre of the shape, fat side down, then lift and mould the petals around it, overlapping them. Add three more sets of petals. On the final set, roll each petal outwards to give an open rose. Allow to dry.

4 Roll out the white sugarpaste to around 2mm (¹⁄₁₆in) thick and cut a 10cm (4in) circle. Moisten the underside with a damp paintbrush and fix on top of the whoopie, smoothing down the sides. Attach the rose in the centre with edible glue.

for the leaves

1 Roll out the green sugarpaste very thinly and cut two leaves, pressing down firmly with the cutter to transfer the vein marks.

2 Scrunch up the foil and place the leaves on this to dry in a natural shape. When dry, attach on either side of the rose with edible glue.

Recipes vanilla whoopies, fillings *Techniques* rolling out sugarpaste, cutting out shapes, frilling

prima ballerina

●●●

Every little girl loves ballet, so why not make this ballerina for your special girl?

you will need...

- filled whoopie pie (flavour of your choice)
- petal paste: 50g (1¾oz) pink
- sugarpaste: 15g (½oz) pink, 8g (¼oz) flesh
- 5ml (1 tsp) CMC (Tylo)
- royal icing in piping (pastry) bags: 15ml (1 tbsp) white with no. 2 tube (tip); 15ml (1 tbsp) pale yellow with no. 11 tube (tip)
- edible dust: white, blue and black
- 15cm (6in) piece of dry spaghetti
- garrett frill cutter and cocktail stick (toothpick)

for the tutu

1 Roll out the petal paste thinly and cut a circle with a Garrett frill cutter. Frill the edges with a cocktail stick.
2 Pipe white royal icing around the top of the whoopie and add the frill.
3 Repeat to create a second frill, removing a 5cm (2in) section to reduce the size. Repeat for the third layer, removing a 10cm (4in) section.

for the body

1 Knead 2.5ml (½ tsp) CMC (Tylo) into the pink sugarpaste. Mould into a bodice shape and fix in the centre. Push the spaghetti through the top of the bodice and into the cake, leaving 2cm (¾in) showing at the top.
2 Knead the remaining CMC (Tylo)

into the flesh sugarpaste. Mould 2g (¹⁄₁₆oz) of this into a cone for the neck and shoulders and push down over the spaghetti, leaving 1cm (⅜in) showing to support the head.

for the head and arms

1 Roll 4g (⅛oz) flesh sugarpaste into a ball and push onto the shoulders. Add a tiny nose. Use a piping tube (tip) to indent a mouth.
2 Roll the remaining flesh sugarpaste into a thin sausage 7cm (2¾in) long. Divide into two and fix one arm to each shoulder. Position across the bodice, flattening the hands.
3 Paint the eyes with the edible dusts.
4 Finally, pipe long hair using the pale yellow royal icing.

Recipes whoopies, fillings, royal icing *Techniques* frilling, painting faces, piping hair, making figures

glitter and glamour

Add a touch of sparkle to your party with these sensational shimmering whoopies.

you will need...

- five filled vanilla whoopies
- 250g (8¾oz) extra vanilla buttercream in a piping (pastry) bag with large star tube (tip)
- edible gold leaf
- edible gold and silver stars
- edible silver balls
- white edible glitter

1 Pipe a swirl of vanilla buttercream on top of each whoopie.

2 Sprinkle the whoopies randomly with a selection of edible stars, silver balls, edible glitter and pieces of edible gold leaf.

going for gold...
Gold leaf will stick to your fingers so tweezers are the best tools to use for positioning the pieces.

make it special...
Mix some edible glitter in with the buttercream for the filling to make the whoopies sparkle from head to toe!

Recipes vanilla whoopies, vanilla buttercream *Techniques* piping

spotty and dotty

Polka dots in pastel shades make the cutest whoopies ever – once this little trio has been spotted they won't be around for long!

you will need...

- three filled whoopies (flavour of your choice)
- sugarpaste: 50g (1¾oz) each white, pale blue, pale pink, 5g (⅛oz) pale green
- cutters: 1cm (⅜in) circle, 10cm (4in) circle
- edible glue

1 Roll out the white, pink and blue sugarpaste colours to around 2mm (1/16in) thick and cut one 10cm (4in) circle from each colour, reserving the trimmings.

2 Moisten the undersides with a damp paintbrush and fix on top of the whoopies, smoothing down the sides.

3 Thinly roll out the leftover pink and white sugarpaste and the green sugarpaste and cut around 15 dots from each colour using the 1cm (⅜in) circle cutter.

4 Fix the dots randomly to the top of each whoopie – green on white, pink on blue and white on pink – with a dab of edible glue.

make it special...
Sprinkle the dots with edible glitter before positioning them on the cakes to give extra sparkle to your whoopies.

Recipes whoopies, fillings *Techniques* rolling out sugarpaste, cutting out shapes

very berry

Strawberries and cream are a classic combination – team them with other berries to create a variety of irresistible indulgences.

you will need...

• three vanilla whoopies filled with whipped cream

• 200g (7oz) freshly whipped double cream in a piping (pastry) bag with large star tube (tip)

• selection of fresh seasonal berries

• absorbent kitchen paper

1 Gently wash your fruit and pat dry with absorbent kitchen paper.

2 Pipe a swirl of thick whipped cream on top of the whoopies and decorate with a single strawberry, or groups of other berries as desired.

whip it up...
These whoopies are best eaten immediately, but as they are so simple, you can make them up just before you serve them.

make it special...
Add a layer of strawberry or raspberry jam inside the whoopies for a perfect afternoon tea treat.

Recipes vanilla whoopies *Techniques* piping

country garden

Host the perfect summer garden party, using your favourite pretty cake stand to display all these gorgeous whoopies from the Pretty as a Picture chapter.

you will need...

- six Rosebud Romance whoopies
- six Butterfly Kisses whoopies
- four filled vanilla whoopies
- sugarpaste: 200g (7oz) white
- petal paste: 10g (3/8oz) each pink, purple
- cutters: hydrangea cutter and mould set, 10cm (4in) circle
- royal icing in piping (pastry) bags with no. 2 tubes (tips): 15ml (1 tbsp) each pink, purple
- white edible glitter
- decorative cake stand

1 Roll out the white sugarpaste to around 2mm (1/16in) thick and cut four 10cm (4in) circles. Moisten the undersides with a damp paintbrush and fix on top of the filled whoopies, smoothing down the sides.

2 Roll out the pink petal paste very thinly and cut four hydrangeas. Press each flower between a lightly dusted former and set aside to dry. Attach one to the top of one whoopie and three to the top of another whoopie with a dab of royal icing. Repeat for the purple petal paste. Pipe a large dot in the centre of each flower.

3 Sprinkle with edible glitter and arrange on your cake stand with the Rosebud Romance and Butterfly Kisses whoopies (see separate instructions earlier in this chapter).

make it special...
Display on a white tablecloth scattered with rose petals and surrounded by vases of fresh roses and hydrangeas.

Recipes vanilla whoopies, fillings, royal icing   *Techniques* rolling out sugarpaste, shaping flowers, piping

twinkling tree

Create a little winter wonderland with a forest of these Christmas tree whoopies.

you will need...

- filled whoopie (flavour of your choice)
- sugarpaste: 50g (1¾oz) white, 20g (¾oz) green
- cutters: 10cm (4in) circle, large, medium, small and extra-small stars
- white edible glitter
- 15ml (1 tbsp) white royal icing in a piping (pastry) bag with no. 2 tube (tip)

1 Roll out the white sugarpaste to around 2mm (⅟₁₆in) thick and cut a 10cm (4in) circle. Moisten the underside with a damp paintbrush and fix on top of the whoopie, smoothing down the sides.

2 Roll out the green sugarpaste and cut nine stars – three small, three medium and three large and cut one extra-small star from the white sugarpaste. Set aside to dry.

3 Moisten the white star with a damp paintbrush and sprinkle with white edible glitter.

4 Fix a large star in the centre of the whoopie with a dab of royal icing. Fix a second large star on top of the first, slightly offset, followed by the third. Continue building the tree in this way with the remaining stars.

5 Pipe a dab of royal icing on the top of the tree and place the small white star on top. Pipe small white dots randomly all over the whoopie and sprinkle the tree with edible glitter.

make it special...
Pipe your guest's names on the whoopies and use them as your Christmas Day place settings.

Recipes whoopies, fillings, royal icing *Techniques* rolling out sugarpaste, cutting out shapes, piping

festive fancies

Children will love creating these fun and easy-to-make Christmas whoopies.

you will need...

- three filled whoopies (flavour of your choice)

- sugarpaste: 170g (6oz) white, 20g (¾oz) green, 10g (⅜oz) brown, 5g (⅛oz) red

- cutters: 10cm (4in) circle, 3cm (1⅛in) circle, large Christmas tree, large snowflake, 6 x 4cm (2½ x 1½in) oval

- royal icing in piping (pastry) bags with no. 2 tubes (tips): 15ml (1 tbsp) each orange, red, blue, yellow

- white edible glitter

- black food colour pen

1 Roll out the white sugarpaste to around 2mm (⅟₁₆in) thick and cut three 10cm (4in) circles. Moisten the undersides with a damp paintbrush and fix on top of the whoopies, smoothing down the sides.

2 For the snowflake whoopie Roll out the white trimmings and cut a large snowflake. Moisten with a damp paintbrush and sprinkle with edible glitter. Fix in the centre of a whoopie with a dab of royal icing.

3 For the tree whoopie Roll out the green sugarpaste and cut a tree. Fix in the centre of a whoopie with a dab of royal icing. Pipe baubles with the various royal icing colours.

4 For the reindeer whoopie Roll out the brown sugarpaste and cut out an oval shape for the face. Attach towards the bottom of the final whoopie with a dab of royal icing. Roll out the red sugarpaste and cut a circle for the nose. Fix to the bottom of the oval. Roll a tiny ball from the white sugarpaste trimmings. Flatten and fix to the top right of the nose as a highlight. Draw two dots for eyes with the black food colour pen. Pipe antlers with orange royal icing.

time saver...
Use sprinkles or food colour pens instead of royal icing for the tree baubles.

Recipes whoopies, fillings, royal icing *Techniques* rolling out sugarpaste, cutting out shapes, piping

christmas characters ⚬⚬⚬

Have fun modelling these cute festive figures to adorn some snowy whoopies.

you will need...

• three filled whoopies (flavour of your choice)

• sugarpaste: 200g (7oz) white, 60g (2⅛oz) red, 190g (6¾oz) black, 10g (⅜oz) green, 5g (⅛oz) orange, 5g (⅛oz) yellow, 2g (¹⁄₁₆oz) flesh

• cutters: 10cm (4in) circle, 1.5cm (½in) circle, 1cm (⅜in) heart, 2cm (¾in) teardrop

• white edible glitter

• royal icing in piping (pastry) bags with no. 2 tubes (tips): 30ml (2 tbsp) white; 15ml (1 tbsp) black

• edible glue

1 Cut three 10cm (4in) circles from the white sugarpaste and fix on top of the whoopies in the usual way.

2 For each of the bodies Use 40g (1½oz) of the appropriate colour paste and mould into a skittle shape.

3 For the snowman Roll two white sausages for arms and fix to the sides. Cut a 0.5 x 10cm (⅛ x 4in) strip of yellow, snip tassels into both ends and glue around the neck. Mould a green hat and fix on the head. Roll a small orange nose and fix in place. Pipe black dots for the eyes and buttons. Indent a smile with the end of a piping tube (tip). Attach in the centre of the whoopie.

4 For Santa Roll a thin white belt and attach round the middle. Roll two red sausages for arms and fix to the sides then pipe white cuffs. Cut a 1.5cm (½in) flesh circle for the face. Roll a tiny nose and fix in place. Mould a hat from 10g (⅜oz) red sugarpaste and fix on the head. Pipe the brim, pompom and beard with white royal icing and pipe the eyes and buckle with black royal icing. Attach in the centre of the whoopie.

5 For the penguins Cut two white teardrops and attach to each body. Make beaks and eyes from tiny balls and fix on. Make a scarf and hat from trimmings. Cut four orange hearts for feet. Fix on the whoopie and attach the penguins on top.

6 Spread royal icing in front of each figure and sprinkle with edible glitter.

Recipes whoopies, fillings, royal icing   *Techniques* cutting out shapes, piping, making figures

figgy pudding

For those of you who don't like the traditional rich Christmas pudding, here's a whoopie alternative!

you will need...

- filled chocolate whoopie
- sugarpaste: 50g (1¾oz) brown, 25g (⅞oz) pale yellow, 10g (⅜oz) green, 5g (⅛oz) black, 2g (¹⁄₁₆oz) red
- cutters: 10cm (4in) circle, 3cm (1in) circle, medium holly leaf
- white edible glitter
- edible glue

1 Roll out the brown sugarpaste to around 5mm (⅛in) thick. Sprinkle small balls of black sugarpaste randomly over the brown sugarpaste and roll out again to around 2mm (¹⁄₁₆in) to flatten the balls and incorporate them.

2 Cut out a 10cm (4in) circle, moisten the underside with a damp paintbrush and fix on top of the whoopie, smoothing down the sides.

3 Roll out the pale yellow sugarpaste and cut a splat shape for the custard. Fix in the centre of the whoopie with a dab of edible glue.

4 Roll out the green sugarpaste and cut three holly leaves, pressing down firmly with the cutter to transfer the vein marks. Position evenly on top of the custard and fix with a dab of edible glue. Roll three berries from the red sugarpaste and fix in the centre of the leaves.

make it special...
Adorn the whoopie with sparklers for a bit of festive pizzazz!

Recipes chocolate whoopies, fillings *Techniques* rolling out sugarpaste, cutting out shapes

swan lake

These incredibly special little cakes will cause a sensation at any gathering.

you will need...

- filled vanilla whoopie
- sugarpaste: 75g (2½oz) white
- 2.5ml (½ tsp) CMC (Tylo)
- food colour pens: orange, black
- three clear mints
- 15ml (1 tbsp) white royal icing in a piping (pastry) bag with no. 2 tube (tip)
- extra 15ml (1 tbsp) white royal icing
- 10cm (4in) circle cutter
- 2.5ml (½ tsp) piping gel coloured blue
- white edible glitter

for the swan

1 Add 2.5ml (½ tsp) CMC (Tylo) to 25g (⅞oz) white sugarpaste. Set 6g (¼oz) aside, and shape the remainder into a teardrop shape for the body. Snip 'feathers' into the body with scissors. Allow to dry.

2 Use half the sugarpaste set aside in step 1 to shape the neck, then roll out the other half and cut out two wing shapes. Snip feathers into the wings. Allow to dry.

3 Draw on the eyes and beak with food colour pens. Secure the wings and neck to the body with a dab of royal icing.

for the lake

1 Place the mints close together on baking parchment in a medium oven for 10 minutes, or until melted together. Allow to cool and harden.

2 Roll out the remaining sugarpaste and cut a 10cm (4in) circle. Moisten and fix on top of the whoopie, smoothing down the sides.

3 Spread the blue piping gel in the centre of the whoopie to form the lake, then position the hardened mints on top and push down gently.

4 Use 15ml (1 tbsp) royal icing to cover the edges of the mint and rough up the surface with the back of a knife. Use a dab of royal icing to fix the swan to the centre of the lake. Sprinkle with white edible glitter.

Recipes vanilla whoopies, fillings, royal icing   *Techniques* rolling out sugarpaste, colouring, piping

fir-tree extravaganza

Make your Christmas party all the more special with this stunning whoopie tree complete with fairy, for the centrepiece of your festive table.

you will need...

- 22 green whoopies filled with green buttercream
- Prima Ballerina whoopie (see Pretty as a Picture – in white, not pink)
- sugarpaste: 1.25kg (2lb 12oz) green
- petal paste: 30g (1oz) white
- cutters: 10cm (4in) fluted circle, small arum lily, small star
- edible glitter: green, white, gold
- wire cupcake stand
- 5cm (2in) piece of dry spaghetti
- rice paper

1 For the tree Roll out the sugarpaste to around 2mm (¹⁄₁₆in) thick and cut out 22 fluted circles. Moisten the undersides and fix on top of the whoopies, smoothing down the sides. Sprinkle with green glitter and arrange on the stand.

2 For the baubles Thinly roll out the petal paste and cut 22 baubles using the arum lily cutter. Moisten and sprinkle with gold edible glitter. Allow to dry then fix to the fronts of the whoopies with edible glue.

3 For the fairy's crown Take the Prima Ballerina whoopie and after piping her hair, cut a strip of leftover petal paste measuring 3 x 0.5cm (1⅛ x ⅛in). Cut a zigzag along the top edge, moisten and sprinkle with white edible glitter, bend into a circle and place on top of the fairy's head.

4 For the wand Cut two stars from leftover petal paste and sandwich together around one end of the spaghetti. Moisten and dip into white edible glitter. Once dry, fix in the fairy's hand with edible glue and push the bottom of the wand into the skirt to secure it.

5 For the wings Cut out a heart shape around 3cm (1⅛in) wide from the rice paper. Fold in half and stick to the back of the fairy with edible glue. Sprinkle the dress and bodice with white edible glitter. Position the fairy at the top of the cupcake stand.

Recipes whoopies, buttercream, royal icing   *Techniques* cutting out shapes, colouring, piping

happy halloween

Cook up these special Halloween whoopies to delight your trick or treaters! All you need are orange and black coloured whoopies, a box of Halloween cutters, a bit of royal icing and a large sprinkling of bright orange edible glitter – magic!

flying broomstick

Model a quick broomstick – mark the bristles with a sharp knife and away you fly…

spooky ghost

A ghoulish treat, made simply by piping a scary mouth and eyes with black royal icing.

witch's cat

With its yellow staring eyes, this cat looks really wicked!

vampire bat

A bat design is made all the more spooky by piping two red fangs – bloodsuckingly good!

perfect pumpkin

Forget the pumpkin carving contest, why not have a competition to see who can pipe the scariest pumpkin face?

bonfire night

Set your table alight with these explosive whoopies!

you will need...

- three filled chocolate whoopies

- sugarpaste: 100g (3½oz) yellow, 50g (1¾oz) brown, 20g (¾oz) green, 5g (⅛oz) orange, 2g (¹⁄₁₆oz) each black, blue

- 10cm (4in) circle cutter

- ten chocolate sticks

- mini marshmallows

- royal icing in piping (pastry) bags with no. 2 tubes (tips): 15ml (1 tbsp) each red, orange, yellow

- white edible glitter

- edible glue

1 Roll out the yellow and brown sugarpastes to around 2mm (¹⁄₁₆in) thick and cut two 10cm (4in) circles from the yellow paste and one from the brown. Moisten the undersides with a damp paintbrush and fix on top of the whoopies, smoothing down the sides.

2 For the bonfire whoopie Break the chocolate sticks into pieces around 6cm (2½in) long. Pile in the centre of the brown whoopie, sticking together with dabs of red, orange and yellow royal icing for the flames. Scatter with mini marshmallows.

3 For the rocket whoopie Roll out the red sugarpaste and cut a rectangle around 3 x 1.5cm (1 x ½in). Roll out the black sugarpaste and cut a 1.5cm (½in) triangle. Fix towards the top of the whoopie with a dab of edible glue. Pipe swirly lines coming from the bottom of the rocket, using red, orange and yellow royal icing. Sprinkle with white edible glitter.

4 For the Catherine wheel whoopie Roll the green sugarpaste into a thin sausage around 30cm (12in) long and roll up to make the wheel. Fix to the whoopie with a dab of edible glue. Make the touch paper by moulding a small rectangle from blue sugarpaste and fixing to the end of the wheel. Pipe red motion lines around the wheel and sprinkle with white edible glitter.

Recipes chocolate whoopies, fillings, royal icing   *Techniques* rolling out sugarpaste, piping

easter goodies

Ring the changes this year – give whoopies instead of Easter eggs!

you will need...

• three filled whoopies (flavour of your choice)

• sugarpaste: 150g (5¼oz) white, 10g (⅜oz) yellow, 5g (⅛oz) blue, 2g (¹⁄₁₆oz) orange

• cutters: 10cm (4in) circle, 6 x 4cm (2½ x 1½in) oval

• one shredded wheat cereal (25g/⅞oz)

• 40g (1½oz) chocolate

• royal icing in piping (pastry) bags with no. 2 tubes (tips): 15ml (1 tbsp) each orange, yellow

• mini chocolate eggs

• black food colour pen

1 Roll out the white sugarpaste to around 2mm (¹⁄₁₆in) thick and cut three 10cm (4in) circles. Moisten the undersides with a damp paintbrush and fix on top of the whoopies, smoothing down the sides.

2 For the chicks whoopie Break up the chocolate and melt in a microwave, then crumble the shredded wheat into the bowl and coat all the strands. Place in two mounds on greaseproof paper, indenting the centres to form nests. Set aside to harden. Use 6g (¼oz) yellow sugarpaste to make one small and one large teardrop shape. Roll two yellow balls and fix to the wide end of each teardrop. Draw on the eyes and attach a tiny orange

beak. When the nests are dry, place the two chicks inside one nest and fix on top of the first whoopie.

3 For the nest of eggs whoopie Fill the second chocolate nest with the chocolate mini eggs and fix on top of the next whoopie.

4 For the Easter egg whoopie Roll out the blue sugarpaste and cut an oval shape. Roll two thin flat sausages using the orange and yellow sugarpaste. For each strip, cut one long side straight and the other in a zigzag. Transfer to the egg and fix in place, trimming any excess paste. Pipe wavy lines and a large dot in orange and yellow royal icing at either end of the egg. Attach to the top of the final whoopie.

Recipes whoopies, fillings, royal icing *Techniques* rolling out sugarpaste, cutting out shapes, piping

blissful babies

Who can resist these beautiful babes? Perfect for a baby shower or christening.

you will need...

- **three filled whoopies** (flavour of your choice)

- **sugarpaste:** 150g (5¼oz) white, 80g (2¾oz) pink, 40g (1½oz) blue, 30g (1oz) flesh, 1g (¹⁄₁₆oz) brown

- **10cm (4in) circle cutter**

- **decal-edge cutting wheel**

- **royal icing in piping (pastry) bags with no. 2 tubes (tips):** 5ml (1 tsp) each yellow, black

- **edible glitter:** blue, pink

- **black food colour pen**

- **edible glue**

1 Roll out the white sugarpaste to around 2mm (¹⁄₁₆in) thick and cut out three 10cm (4in) circles. Moisten the undersides with a damp paintbrush and fix on top of the whoopies, smoothing down the sides.

2 Put 2g (¹⁄₁₆oz) of the flesh sugarpaste aside and divide the remainder into three to make three raised oval shapes for the heads. Fix the heads to the top of each whoopie with a dab of edible glue, and use the remaining paste to make three tiny noses and six small ears.

3 Cut two pink and one blue circle using the 10cm (4in) cutter. Cut across the top third of each circle using a decal-edge cutting wheel and use the larger section of each circle to make the blankets. Moisten with a damp paintbrush and sprinkle liberally with glitter. Lay across the whoopie just below the head, fixing in place using a damp paintbrush.

4 Use scraps of the pink and blue sugarpaste to make two dummies and position where the mouths should be. For the last baby, indent a smile with the wide end of a piping tube (tip) and fix a tiny piece of white sugarpaste to the bottom of the smile for a tooth.

5 Draw on the eyes with the black food colour pen. Pipe hair using yellow and black royal icing onto two of the babies' heads and use a tiny piece of brown sugarpaste to make hair for the final baby.

Recipes whoopies, fillings, royal icing *Techniques* rolling out sugarpaste, cutting out shapes, piping hair

birthday balloons

These whoopies piled up high on a cake stand look absolutely amazing!
Primary colours look great but you can make them in any shades.

you will need...

• three filled whoopies (flavour of your choice)

• sugarpaste: 150g (5¼oz) white, 18g (¾oz) red, 12g (½oz) blue, 10g (⅜oz) orange, 2g (¹⁄₁₆oz) yellow

• cutters: 10cm (4in) circle, medium oval

• royal icing in piping (pastry) bags with no. 2 tubes (tips): 15ml (1 tbsp) each orange, yellow

• edible glue

• coloured sprinkles

1 Roll out the white sugarpaste to around 2mm (¹⁄₁₆in) thick and cut out three 10cm (4in) circles. Moisten the undersides with a damp paintbrush and fix on top of the whoopies, smoothing down the sides.

2 For the gifts whoopie Mould 10g (⅜oz) each of blue, red and orange sugarpaste into cubes and rectangular prisms for the parcels. Fix to a whoopie with dabs of edible glue. Pipe ribbon and a bow on each parcel with yellow royal icing.

3 For the balloons whoopie Thinly roll out 2g (1¹⁄₁₆oz) each of blue, yellow and red sugarpaste and cut three oval shapes. Fix towards the top of one whoopie with a dab of edible glue. From the trimmings, cut three small triangles (one of each colour) and fix at the base of each balloon for the knots. Use the orange royal icing to pipe strings from the knot to the base of the whoopie.

4 For the candles whoopie Roll the remaining orange sugarpaste into three thin sausages around 5cm (2in) long. Trim both ends to make them straight. Fix to the remaining whoopie with dabs of edible glue. Pipe flames using the yellow royal icing. Sprinkle all the whoopies with colourful sprinkles or glue on tiny balls of coloured sugarpaste.

Recipes whoopies, fillings, royal icing *Techniques* rolling out sugarpaste, cutting out shapes, piping

13

pool party

This stunning pool table will be a real talking point at any special celebration and would be a great birthday cake for men, who are always difficult to design for.

you will need...

• 16 vanilla whoopie pies, filled with vanilla buttercream

• 100g (3½oz) extra vanilla buttercream

• 75 x 45cm (30 x 18in) cake board

• sugarpaste: 3kg (6lb 10oz) dark green, 515g (1lb 2⅛oz) white, 130g (4½oz) light brown, 110g (3⅞oz) blue, 95g (3⅜oz) black, 60g (2oz) each of yellow, blue, red, purple, orange, green and brown

• 15ml (3 tsp) CMC (Tylo)

• royal icing in piping (pastry) bags with no. 2 tubes (tips): 30ml (2 tbsp) each white, black

• cutters: 10cm (4in) circle, 8cm (3in) circle, 5cm (2in) circle and 3cm (1¼in) circle

• edible glue

for the table

1 Roll out the dark green sugarpaste to around 2mm (⅟₁₆in) thick and cover the cake board.

2 Knead the CMC (Tylo) into 1kg (2lb 3¼oz) of the trimmings. Divide into two portions of 300g (10½oz) for the long sides of the table and two portions of 200g (7oz) for the short sides. Roll each portion into a sausage approximately 1.5cm (½in) thick. Flatten the top and sides using smoothers. Mitre both ends to form the corners. Attach around the edges of the board with edible glue.

keep it clean...
Wash your hands and clean the surface and rolling pin thoroughly between each colour change to avoid spoiling the clean look of the finished balls.

3 Roll out 30g (1oz) black sugarpaste to around 2mm (¹⁄₁₆in) thick and cut one 8cm (3in) circle and one 5cm (2in) circle. Cut the larger circle into quarters and cut the smaller circle in half.

4 Use edible glue to stick the quarter circles into each of the corners and the semicircles halfway down each of the long sides to make the pockets. Use the white royal icing to pipe the nets.

for the balls

1 Roll out 500g (1lb 1½oz) white sugarpaste to around 2mm (¹⁄₁₆in) thick and cut eight 10cm (4in) circles. Spread a thin layer of buttercream on top of eight whoopies and cover with the white discs, smoothing down the sides. Repeat with the coloured sugarpastes for the remaining eight whoopies.

2 Cut fifteen 3.5cm (1¼in) circles from the remaining white sugarpaste. Fix eight of these in the centre of each of the coloured balls with edible glue.

3 Roll each of the remaining coloured pastes (apart from the black) into rectangles measuring approximately 3.5 x 15cm (1¼ x 6in). Fix across the centre of each of the white balls with edible glue, trimming where necessary. Fix the remaining seven white circles in the centre of each coloured strip. Leave the final ball white for the cue ball.

4 With the black royal icing, pipe the numbers 1–8 on the coloured balls, and 9–15 on the balls with stripes. Fix the balls in position on the table with a dab of buttercream.

for the cue and chalk

1 Knead 5ml (1 tsp) of CMC (Tylo) into the light brown sugarpaste. Roll into a long sausage, thinning at one end.

2 To make the tip of the cue, roll 15g (½oz) of white sugarpaste into a short sausage around 1cm (³⁄₈in) long and the same thickness as the thin end of the cue. Attach using a dab of royal icing. Roll 5g (¹⁄₈oz) of black sugarpaste into a ball and flatten between your thumb and forefinger. Attach to the white tip with a dab of royal icing.

3 Mould 50g (1¾oz) of blue sugarpaste into a cube and indent the top with your thumb to form the chalk. Position on the edge of the table.

make it special...
For extra wow factor, bake the whoopies in vibrant colours.

Recipes   vanilla whoopies, buttercream, royal icing   *Techniques*   cutting out shapes, piping, colouring

be my valentine

Here's a wonderful way to surprise your special someone – with these gorgeous romantic whoopies. They are so simple to make – just roll out the sugarpaste, cut lots of hearts and kisses and sprinkle liberally with edible glitter!

hot lips

Cut a voluptuous pair of lips using a very sharp craft knife and glitter copiously.

heart's desire

Let these hearts dry hard before pushing them gently into the top of your whoopie.

confetti coeurs

Punch out lots of tiny hearts, moisten the top of the whoopie and scatter – not forgetting to glitter afterwards!

cupid's arrow

Pipe an arrow through the centre of a glittered heart for a classic romantic whoopie.

heart to heart

This pale pink heart whoopie is the perfect dessert for your loved one on Valentine's Day – how could they resist?

marry me?

If your girlfriend likes bling, she'll love this sparkly engagement ring whoopie.

you will need...

- filled whoopie (flavour of your choice)
- sugarpaste: 50g (1¾oz) white
- cocktail stick (toothpick)
- 10cm (4in) circle cutter
- edible glitter: silver, white
- 15ml (1 tbsp) white royal icing in a piping (pastry) bag with no. 2 tube (tip)

1 Roll out the white sugarpaste to around 2mm (⅟₁₆in) thick and cut a 10cm (4in) circle. Moisten the underside with a damp paintbrush and fix on top of the whoopie, smoothing down the sides.

2 Roll 1g (⅟₁₆oz) of leftover sugarpaste into a ball and skewer it on the end of a cocktail stick (toothpick). Moisten the ball and dip into the silver edible glitter. Leave to dry.

3 Roll the remaining sugarpaste into a long thin sausage, moisten and roll in the white edible glitter. Bend into a circle and place on top of the whoopie with the join at the front. Attach the sparkly ball on top of the join with a dab of royal icing.

hold steady...
Use a small mound of sugarpaste to hold the cocktail stick (toothpick) upright while the glittered ball dries.

Recipes whoopies, fillings, royal icing *Techniques* rolling out sugarpaste, cutting out shapes, piping

top hat and tiara

●●●

These fun and elegant whoopies are a great twist on the traditional bride and groom designs and will make a fantastic addition to anyone's special day.

you will need...

- two filled vanilla whoopies
- sugarpaste: 100g (3½oz) white, 10g (⅜oz) black
- cutters: 10cm (4in) circle, 3cm (1in) circle
- 15ml (1 tbsp) white royal icing in a piping (pastry) bag with no. 2 tube (tip)
- baking parchment
- white edible glitter

1 For the bow tie Use 2g (¹⁄₁₆oz) black sugarpaste to make two triangles with a ball in the centre.

2 For the top hat Cut a 3cm (1in) circle from the remaining black sugarpaste to form the brim, and mould the rest into a tube for the top. Fix the top in the centre of the brim with a dab of royal icing. Allow to dry.

3 For the tiara Roll the baking parchment into a cylindrical shape around 3cm (1in) diameter and secure with tape – this ensures that the tiara will dry curved. Pipe a design onto the parchment to form the tiara and allow to dry overnight. Once dry, carefully slip the tiara off

the parchment, moisten the front with a damp paintbrush and sprinkle with white edible glitter.

4 Roll out the white sugarpaste to around 2mm (¹⁄₁₆in) thick and cut two 10cm (4in) circles. Moisten the undersides with a damp paintbrush and fix on top of the whoopies, smoothing down the sides.

5 Secure the top hat and bow tie to one whoopie with dabs of royal icing. Secure the tiara to the second whoopie by piping a thin line of royal icing along the base of the tiara, and pressing on very gently. Pipe dots around the edge of the whoopie and sprinkle with white edible glitter.

Recipes vanilla whoopies, fillings, royal icing *Techniques* rolling out sugarpaste, piping

happy anniversary

Don't let milestone wedding anniversaries go by without making these glittering whoopies to mark the occasion.

you will need...

- **three filled whoopies** (flavour of your choice)
- sugarpaste: 150g (5¼oz) white
- petal paste: 15g (½oz) white
- cutters: 10cm (4in) circle, numbers
- edible glitter: red, gold, white
- edible glue

1 Roll out the white sugarpaste to around 2mm (¹⁄₁₆in) thick and cut three 10cm (4in) circles. Moisten the undersides with a damp paintbrush and fix on top of the whoopies, smoothing down the sides.

2 Cut out the numbers needed (for a silver wedding, a 2 and a 5, for a ruby wedding, a 4 and a 0, and for a golden wedding, a 5 and a 0). Moisten each number with a damp paintbrush, cover with the appropriate coloured edible glitter and allow to dry for two minutes.

3 Position the pairs of numbers on top of the whoopies, securing each with a dab of edible glue.

make it special...
Create a 3D display by cutting two of each number and gluing together either side of a wire.

Recipes whoopies, fillings *Techniques* rolling out sugarpaste, cutting out shapes, using wires

love hearts

Whether it's Valentine's Day or the day you first use the 'L' word, these decorative heart whoopies are the ideal way to mark the occasion.

you will need...

- three filled whoopies (flavour of your choice)

- sugarpaste: 150g (5¼oz) white

- petal paste: 15g (½oz) in three shades of pink

- cutters: 10cm (4in) circle, 6cm (2½in) heart

- white edible glitter

- 15ml (1 tbsp) pink royal icing in a piping (pastry) bag with no. 1.5 tube (tip)

1 Roll out the white sugarpaste to around 2mm (⅟₁₆in) thick and cut three 10cm (4in) circles. Moisten the undersides with a damp paintbrush and fix on top of the whoopies, smoothing down the sides.

2 Cut out three hearts from the petal paste, one from each shade of pink. Set aside to dry. Pipe random lines and swirls on each heart with the pink royal icing.

3 Fix one heart to the top of each whoopie with a dab of royal icing and sprinkle with white edible glitter.

perfect finish...
When piping, don't stop at the edges but sweep over the sides, then clean up the edges with your finger.

long-stemmed rose

Long-stemmed roses are such a romantic offering. Try making this beautiful bouquet – which tastes as good as it looks!

you will need...

- filled whoopie (flavour of your choice)
- sugarpaste: 50g (1¾oz) white
- petal paste: 6g (¼oz) dark red
- 10cm (4in) circle cutter
- 15ml (1 tbsp) green royal icing in a piping (pastry) bag with no. 2 tube (tip)
- red edible glitter

1 Roll out the white sugarpaste to around 2mm (¹⁄₁₆in) thick and cut a 10cm (4in) circle. Moisten the underside with a damp paintbrush and fix on top of the whoopie, smoothing down the sides.

2 Roll out the petal paste very thinly. Cut three strips each measuring 1 x 6cm (⅜ x 2⅜in). Gently flatten one long side of each strip with a rolling pin to thin it. Roll up each strip (flattened edge uppermost) to form a little rose, pinching the bottom end to form a point. Allow to dry for a couple of hours or overnight.

3 Moisten the roses with a damp paintbrush then dip into the red edible glitter. Set aside for a couple of minutes to dry. Position all three roses towards the top of the whoopie, securing with a dab of royal icing. Pipe long stems from the bottom of each rose and pipe small leaves down the length of the stem.

for open roses... While rolling each rose, use your thumb to push out the top gently.

chocolate temptation

This indulgent quartet of whoopies is a chocoholic's dream – the only question is, which one to eat first?

you will need...

• four chocolate whoopies filled with marshmallow cream

• 200g (7oz) chocolate ganache

• chocolate shavings

• two chocolate sticks

• three chocolate truffles

• two cigarette russe biscuits

1 Carefully spread the chocolate ganache on top of the whoopies.

2 Decorate one whoopie with chocolate shavings, another with chocolate sticks, another with the truffles and the final whoopie with the biscuits, as shown.

make it special...
For a fancy flourish, melt some white chocolate and drizzle it over the top.

Recipes   chocolate whoopies, marshmallow cream filling, chocolate ganache topping

hen night

Make a hen party great fun by decorating your whoopies with all things girly – shoes, handbags, lipsticks, hairdryers, corsets... the possibilities are endless! Make the shapes with cutters and decorate with edible paint and lots of glitter!

l-plates

Amuse the bride with these fun L-plates. Just pipe or cut out an 'L' and fix to a square of white sugarpaste.

killer heels

The higher the better! These gorgeous cut-out shoes are sure to delight all the ladies at the party.

blow dryer

Don't forget this essential piece of equipment for your girls' night out!

get lippy

Vampish red or baby pink? Colour this lipstick to match the bride's usual style.

champagne celebration ●●

What better way to toast an engagement, marriage or anniversary than with this bubbly champagne flute whoopie, washed down with a glass of fizz?

you will need...

- filled whoopie (flavour of your choice)
- sugarpaste: 50g (1¾oz) white
- petal paste: 5g (⅛oz) white
- 10cm (4in) circle cutter
- 15ml (1 tbsp) white royal icing in a piping (pastry) bag with no. 2 tube (tip)
- yellow edible glitter
- gold lustre dust

1 Roll out the white sugarpaste to around 2mm (¹⁄₁₆in) thick and cut a 10cm (4in) circle. Moisten the underside with a damp paintbrush and fix on top of the whoopie, smoothing down the sides.

2 Thinly roll out the petal paste and cut two flute shapes by hand. Allow to dry for at least an hour.

3 Cover the top part of the flutes with a piece of paper. Moisten the rest of the flutes with a damp paintbrush and sprinkle with yellow edible glitter. Fix to the top of the whoopie with a dab of royal icing.

4 Pipe tiny dots of royal icing above the flutes to make the bubbles. Allow to dry for ten minutes or so then paint the bubbles gold with the gold lustre dust.

make a template...
To get both the flutes the same, make a cardboard template and cut around it with a craft knife.

Recipes whoopies, fillings, royal icing *Techniques* cutting out shapes, piping, painting

tiers of joy

This elegant tower of whoopie pies makes a fun and innovative alternative to a traditional wedding cake and will serve 50 guests.

you will need...

- 48 filled vanilla whoopies
- Top Hat and Tiara whoopies
- sugarpaste: 3kg (6lb 10oz) white
- cutters: 10cm (4in) circle, small heart, medium heart
- white edible glitter
- 30ml (2 tbsp) white royal icing in a piping (pastry) bag with no. 2 tube (tip)
- three silver floral wires cut in half
- posy pick
- acrylic cake stand

1 Roll out the sugarpaste to around 2mm (1/16in) thick and cut out 48 circles. Moisten the undersides with a damp paintbrush and fix on top of the whoopies, smoothing down the sides.

2 Roll out the trimmings and cut out 47 medium hearts and 10 small hearts. Allow to dry for at least half an hour.

3 Moisten the medium hearts with a damp paintbrush and sprinkle liberally with edible glitter. Set one whoopie aside and fix the hearts in the centre of all the remaining whoopies with a dab of royal icing.

4 Apply edible glue to the underside of five small hearts. Lay the end of a wire in the centre of each heart and sandwich with another heart. Push a posy pick into the centre of the reserved whoopie and insert the wired hearts. Use a tiny ball of sugarpaste to cover the hole at the top of the pick.

5 Arrange the whoopies on the cake stand, placing the wired whoopie and the Top Hat and Tiara whoopies (see instructions earlier in this chapter) on the top tier.

Recipes vanilla whoopies, fillings, royal icing   *Techniques* cutting out shapes, piping, using wires

child's play

noughts and crosses

What a fun way to play an old game – as a prize the winner gets to eat the whoopies!

you will need...

• 30cm (12in) square cake board

• three vanilla whoopies filled with vanilla buttercream

• two black whoopies filled with black buttercream

• sugarpaste: 350g (12⅜oz) white, 350g (12⅜oz) black

• 10cm (4in) circle cutter

• edible glue

1 Roll out 250g (8¾oz) black sugarpaste to around 2mm (¹⁄₁₆in) thick and cut five 10cm (4in) squares. Roll out 200g (7oz) white sugarpaste to around 2mm (¹⁄₁₆in) thick and cut four 10cm (4in) squares.

2 Moisten the cake board and position the squares side by side on the board, starting with a black square and alternating the colours.

3 Roll out the remaining white sugarpaste to around 2mm (¹⁄₁₆in) thick and cut three 10cm (4in) circles. Moisten the undersides with a damp paintbrush and fix on top of the vanilla whoopies, smoothing down

the sides. Repeat with the black sugarpaste for the black whoopies.

4 Use the sugarpaste trimmings to cut six black strips to make three crosses. Fix to the top of the white whoopies with edible glue. Use the white trimmings to form two noughts and fix these to the black whoopies. Position on the board on contrasting squares.

make it fun... Make extra whoopies and use them to play real games of noughts and crosses!

Recipes vanilla whoopies, buttercream *Techniques* colouring, rolling out sugarpaste, cutting out shapes

94 child's play

teddy bear

If you go down to the woods today, don't forget to pack some tasty teddy bear whoopies for your picnic.

you will need...

- one filled and one unfilled chocolate whoopie
- 50g (1¾oz) chocolate buttercream
- sugarpaste: 130g (4½oz) brown, 2g (¹⁄₁₆oz) black
- cutters: 7cm (2¾in) circle, 9cm (3½in) circle, 10cm (4in) circle
- small foam pieces
- two 2.5cm (1in) pieces of dry spaghetti
- 15ml (1 tbsp) black royal icing in a piping (pastry) bag with no. 2 tube (tip)

for the head

1 Cut a 7cm (2¾in) circle from each half of the unfilled whoopie. Sandwich together with buttercream.
2 Roll out the brown sugarpaste to around 2mm (¹⁄₁₆in) thick and cut a 9cm (3½in) circle. Moisten the underside and fix on top of the whoopie, smoothing down the sides.
3 Shape two ears from 8g (¼oz) brown sugarpaste. Push the spaghetti pieces halfway into the head, at an angle. Apply edible glue and push the ears onto the spaghetti. Support with small foam pieces until dry.
4 Roll two eyes from black sugarpaste and mould a triangle for the nose. Fix in position and pipe the mouth.

for the body

1 Cover the filled whoopie with a 10cm (4in) brown circle as before.
2 Use 10g (⅜oz) brown sugarpaste to mould a foot with four pads. Make another foot (reversed) and fix to the bottom of the whoopie.
3 Divide the remaining brown paste and roll two sausages 1cm (⅜in) thick and 3cm (1⅛in) long. Flatten the ends and fix to the sides for arms. Mark claws with a knife. Position the whoopies side by side.

make it special...
Make a whole family of bears and position them on a green board with lots of flowers.

Recipes chocolate whoopies, chocolate buttercream *Techniques* cutting out shapes, piping

smiley face

The classic bright-yellow happy face is guaranteed to cheer everyone up.

you will need...

- yellow vanilla whoopie filled with yellow buttercream

- sugarpaste: 50g (1¾oz) yellow, 6g (¼oz) black

- cutters: 1cm (⅜in) circle, 10cm (4in) circle

- edible glue

1 Roll out the yellow sugarpaste to around 2mm (⅛in) thick and cut a 10cm (4in) circle. Moisten the underside with a damp paintbrush and fix on top of the whoopie, smoothing down the sides.

2 Roll out 2g (¹⁄₁₆oz) black sugarpaste and cut two 1cm (⅜in) circles for the eyes. Secure to the whoopie with a dab of edible glue.

3 Roll the remaining sugarpaste into a thin sausage and fix to the whoopie in the shape of a smiley mouth with a dab of edible glue.

make it different...
Vary the expression by changing the shape of the eyes and mouth and adding eyebrows, a moustache or a beauty spot.

Recipes vanilla whoopies, buttercream *Techniques* colouring, rolling out sugarpaste, cutting out shapes

under the sea

This tropical sea filled with colourful fish is great for any celebration where children will be present. You can make as many fish as you like – one for each guest.

you will need...

- 12 blue mini whoopies filled with blue buttercream
- three vanilla whoopies coloured red, orange and yellow filled with red, orange and yellow buttercream
- 50 x 45cm (20 x 18in) cake board
- sugarpaste: 2kg 25g (4½lb) white, 50g (1¾oz) each pale brown (not fully mixed), red, green, yellow, orange, 25g (⅞oz) black
- petal paste: 50g (1¾oz) grey, 10g (⅜oz) each orange, yellow, red
- 50g (1¾oz) brown sugar
- blue paste food colour
- edible glitter: white, green
- edible pearl lustre spray
- royal icing in piping (pastry) bags with no. 2 tubes (tips): 15ml (1 tbsp) each white, black
- 10cm (4in) circle cutter
- sea creatures mould

1 For the background Add blue paste food colour to 2kg (4lb 6½oz) white sugarpaste and knead briefly to give a marbled effect. Cover the board with the sugarpaste. Brush edible glue across the bottom 5cm (2in) of the board in a wavy pattern and sprinkle with brown sugar. Sprinkle the board sparingly with white edible glitter.

2 For the sprats Roll out the grey petal paste very thinly and cut out 12 sprat shapes. Place them onto absorbent kitchen paper and spray with edible pearl lustre spray. Leave to dry, then fix to the top of the mini whoopies with dabs of royal icing. Arrange on the board in a shoal and fix in place with royal icing.

3 For the three large fish Roll out the red, orange and yellow sugarpaste to around 2mm (⅟₁₆in) thick and cut one 10cm (4in) circle from each colour. Moisten the undersides with a damp paintbrush and fix on top of the same-coloured whoopies, smoothing down the sides.

4 Thinly roll out the orange, yellow and red petal pastes and cut a tail and fins for each fish. Set aside to dry then push into the buttercream. For the eye, mould a small piece of white sugarpaste into a flat circle and fix in place with edible glue. Pipe a dot of black royal icing in the centre. For the lips, mould a small piece of sugarpaste the same colour as the fish into a sausage shape 1cm (⅜in) long. Bend in the centre and fix in place with edible glue.

5 For the orange fish Roll out the white sugarpaste. Cut one 10 x 0.6cm (4 x ¼in) strip and moisten the underside. Lay this vertically across the fish towards the front of the whoopie. Cut a second strip the same length, but with a more bulbous side, and fix parallel to the first strip. Cut a third smaller strip and fix over the tail. Pipe around the outline of all the white shapes with black royal icing.

6 For the yellow fish Roll out the black sugarpaste and cut three wavy strips 10 x 0.6cm (4 x ¼in). Moisten the undersides and lay these vertically across the fish at regular intervals.

7 For the red fish Pipe small white dots all over the fish.

8 For the shells Use the mould and the pale brown sugarpaste to make lots of different shells and starfish. Scatter on the sand.

9 For the seaweed Roll out the green sugarpaste and cut into lengths around 13 x 0.6cm (5 x ¼in). Twist loosely and pinch at one end. Moisten all over with a damp paintbrush and sprinkle with green edible glitter. Place on the sand.

make it simple…
Use a round board to make a fish bowl, and fill it with lots of goldfish using fish cutters and orange mini whoopies.

over the rainbow

These fun colourful whoopies will brighten up any party, come rain or shine!

you will need...

- two blue and one yellow vanilla whoopies filled with blue/yellow buttercream

- sugarpaste: 105g (3¾oz) blue, 55g (2oz) yellow, 5g (⅛oz) each red, orange, green, indigo, violet

- petal paste: 20g (¾oz) white

- cutters: 10cm (4in) circle, 2cm (¾in) triangle

- 15ml (1 tbsp) yellow royal icing in a small piping (pastry) bag with no. 2 tube (tip)

- edible glitter: white, gold

1 Cut one yellow and two blue 10cm (4in) circles from the sugarpaste. Moisten the undersides with a damp paintbrush and fix on top of the same-coloured whoopies, smoothing down the sides.

2 For the sun whoopie Thinly roll out the yellow petal paste, cut ten 2cm (¾in) triangles and set aside to dry. Pipe eyes and a smile on top of the whoopie in yellow royal icing. Push the dry triangles into the buttercream around the edge of the whoopie.

3 For the rainbow whoopie Roll out and cut a strip from each sugarpaste colour. Dust a board and lay the red strip down in an arc shape. Moisten the edge and fix the orange strip alongside. Repeat for all the colours. Neaten the ends with a knife. Moisten the top of the whoopie with a damp paintbrush and transfer the rainbow with a palette knife. Roll out the petal paste and cut two large and two small cloud shapes. Moisten and sprinkle with white edible glitter. Attach one large cloud and one small cloud to the rainbow.

4 For the cloud whoopie Cut four thin strips from the petal paste. Moisten with a damp paintbrush and sprinkle with gold edible glitter. Fix one large cloud to the whoopie then attach the sunbeams towards the bottom of the cloud. Fix the small cloud on top to conceal the tops of the sunbeams.

Recipes vanilla whoopies, buttercream, royal icing *Techniques* colouring, cutting out shapes, piping

starry starry night

The moon, stars and planet on these night-sky whoopies will be a hit with any budding astronomers.

you will need...

- three filled whoopies (flavour of your choice)
- sugarpaste: 150g (5¼oz) dark blue
- petal paste: 15g (½oz) white
- cutters: small star, 5cm (2in) circle, 8cm (3⅛in) circle, 10cm (4in) circle
- edible glitter: gold, white
- edible glue

1 Roll out the dark blue sugarpaste to around 2mm (¹⁄₁₆in) thick and cut three 10cm (4in) circles. Moisten the undersides with a damp paintbrush and fix on top of the whoopies, smoothing down the sides.

2 For the planet whoopie Roll out the petal paste very thinly and cut a 5cm (2in) circle. Moisten and sprinkle with white edible glitter. Roll out the remaining petal paste and cut an 8cm (3⅛in) circle. Reposition the circle cutter 1cm (⅜in) up from the bottom of the cut circle and re-cut, leaving a semi-circular band of paste. Bend the two ends inwards, moisten with a damp paintbrush and

sprinkle with gold edible glitter. Slide the white circle inside the gold band and fix in the centre of the whoopie with edible glue.

3 For the moon whoopie Roll out the remaining petal paste very thinly and cut a 5cm (2in) circle. Reposition the circle cutter 1cm (⅜in) up from the bottom of the cut circle and re-cut, leaving a crescent-moon shape. Moisten, sprinkle with white glitter and glue to the top of the whoopie.

4 For the stars whoopie Cut a number of stars from the remaining petal paste, moisten and sprinkle with white glitter. Fix to the top of the whoopie with a dab of edible glue.

Recipes whoopies, fillings *Techniques* rolling out sugarpaste, cutting out shapes

hamburger heaven

This fun design is sure to raise a smile when the first bite reveals it is sweet not savoury! Hamburger and cake rolled into one – what more could anyone ask for?

you will need...

- two vanilla whoopie halves
- 30ml (2 tbsp) chocolate buttercream
- sugarpaste: 30g (1oz) red, 20g (¾oz) green, 20g (¾oz) yellow
- cutters: 6cm (2½in) circle, 6cm (2½in) square
- 15ml (1 tbsp) cream royal icing in a small piping (pastry) bag with no. 2 tube (tip)

1 For the burger Spread a 1.5cm (½in) thickness of chocolate buttercream over the flat side of one whoopie half and smooth the edges.

2 For the lettuce Roll out the green sugarpaste to around 2mm (¹⁄₁₆in) thick and cut a 6cm (2½in) circle. Gently pull the edges out between your thumb and forefinger to thin and soften them. Place on top of the burger with the edges overhanging.

3 For the tomato Roll out the red sugarpaste to around 7mm (¼in) thick and cut a 6cm (2½in) circle. Pipe a small amount of royal icing in the centre of the lettuce and place the tomato on top.

4 For the cheese Roll out the yellow sugarpaste to around 2mm (¹⁄₁₆in) thick and cut a 6cm (2½in) square. Pipe a small amount of royal icing in the centre of the tomato and place the cheese on top, at an angle.

5 For the bun top Pipe a small amount of royal icing in the centre of the cheese and place the other whoopie half on top, flat side down. Press down gently. Pipe 'seeds' of royal icing on the top.

make it special...
For a fast-food feast, make some fries from yellow sugarpaste with a squirt of red royal icing for ketchup!

Recipes   vanilla whoopies, chocolate buttercream, royal icing   *Techniques*   cutting out shapes, piping

animal antics

Make these colourful animal characters for a child's birthday or just to brighten up an otherwise dull day. Why not make a whole farmyard or jungle scene?

busy bee

This bee looks cute on its own but imagine a whole swarm! Cut out the wings with a butterfly cutter and dry them resting over a piece of card.

tortoise treat

This is one tortoise that will not be slow moving! To make the shell, mould irregular shapes of greeny brown sugarpaste and fit together on the tortoise's back.

freddie the frog

Make this frog look really cheeky by drying his tongue in a curved shape before fixing it in his mouth.

miss piggy

This design is so easy to make with some pink sugarpaste – your own greedy piglets can help you to make them before they gobble them up!

friendly faces

These whoopies will create so much excitement at a child's party, as your young guests try to recognize their own faces on your cakes.

you will need...

- three filled whoopies (flavour of your choice)
- sugarpaste: 150g (5¼oz) white, 45g (1½oz) flesh
- 10cm (4in) circle cutter
- face mould
- edible dust: white, blue, brown, black
- 15ml (1 tbsp) royal icing in a piping (pastry) bag with no. 47 (basketweave) tube (tip) in hair colour of your choice
- white edible glitter

1 Roll out the white sugarpaste to around 2mm (1/16in) thick and cut three 10cm (4in) circles. Moisten the undersides with a damp paintbrush and fix on top of the whoopies, smoothing down the sides. Moisten the tops of the whoopies and sprinkle with white edible glitter.

2 For each face Dust the face mould well with icing (confectioners') sugar to prevent sticking. Firmly press 15g (½oz) flesh-coloured sugarpaste into the mould, ensuring the paste gets into all the crevices. Slice off the excess paste with a sharp knife. Gently ease the paste out of the mould and allow to dry for a few

minutes before attaching to the centre of the whoopie with a dab of royal icing.

3 Paint the eyes with the edible dusts in the colour of your choice. Pipe the hair in the style and colour of your choice.

make it special...
Make a face for every guest, then pipe their names on, place in a cellophane bag or box and tie with ribbon for a take-home gift.

Recipes whoopies, fillings, royal icing *Techniques* rolling out sugarpaste, piping hair, painting faces

creepy crawly

This adorable centipede is guaranteed to light up children's faces and make a birthday party truly memorable. She is not only cute, she is tasty too!

you will need...

- 12 green filled mini whoopies
- 35cm (14in) cake board
- sugarpaste: 240g (8½oz) green, 40g (1½oz) red, 20g (¾oz) white
- cutters: 4cm (1½in) circle, mini daisy
- two 5cm (2in) pieces of dry spaghetti
- edible glitter: green, red
- royal icing in piping (pastry) bags with no. 2 tubes (tips): 15ml (1 tbsp) each white, black, yellow
- 90ml (6 tbsp) dark green royal icing
- edible dust: white, blue, black

1 For the background Spread the green royal icing over the board and pat with the blade of a palette knife to create textured grass.

2 For the centipede Roll out the green sugarpaste and cut 12 4cm (1½in) circles. Moisten the undersides with a damp paintbrush and fix on top of the whoopies, smoothing down the sides. Sprinkle with green edible glitter. Arrange on the board in an 'S' shape. Paint the face with edible dusts. Roll two tiny balls of red sugarpaste for the antennae and push onto the end of the spaghetti sticks. Paint the balls with edible glue then dip in red glitter. Push the antennae into the head. Roll a sausage of green sugarpaste around 5mm (⅛in) thick and cut into 22 5cm (2in) lengths to make the legs. Bend each leg and attach two legs to each section of the body with edible glue.

3 For the flowers Roll out the white sugarpaste and cut 10–15 mini daisies. Fix to the board in clusters with royal icing and pipe a dot of yellow royal icing in the centres.

4 For the ladybirds Roll small pieces of red sugarpaste into lozenge shapes. Use black royal icing to pipe heads and spots, and white royal icing to pipe eyes.

Recipes whoopies, fillings, royal icing *Techniques* colouring, piping, painting faces

bumper cars

All the fun of the fair in a few delicious little cakes! Any child would be delighted with this as their party cake, with a car for each guest to take home.

you will need...

- eight coloured whoopies filled with coloured buttercream
- 60cm (24in) square cake board
- sugarpaste: 2.5kg (5½lb) grey, 1kg (2¼lb) black, 1kg (2¼lb) in various bright colours, 56g (2oz) flesh-coloured
- cutters: 2.5cm (1in) circle, 10cm (4in) circle
- dry spaghetti
- royal icing in piping (pastry) bags: with no. 11 tubes (tips): 15ml (1 tbsp) each brown, black, yellow; with no. 2 tubes (tips): various colours
- edible dusts: white, blue, black
- edible glue

for the cars

1 Roll out the grey sugarpaste to around 2mm (¹⁄₁₆in) thick and cover the board. Roll four 250g (8¾oz) portions of black sugarpaste into sausages 1.5cm (½in) thick and 60cm (24in) long and flatten the top and sides. Mitre the corners and attach along the edges of the board with edible glue.

2 Use the cutter to remove a 2.5cm (1in) circle of cake from the top of each filled whoopie, towards the back, to create a seat for the drivers.

3 Roll out the coloured sugarpastes and cut eight 10cm (4in) circles, reserving the trimmings. Moisten the undersides with a damp paintbrush and fix on top of the whoopies, smoothing down the sides.

4 Cut another eight 10cm (4in) circles from the coloured sugarpastes, cut in half and secure a contrasting colour to the front of each whoopie.

5 Make steering wheels by rolling 2g (¹⁄₁₆oz) pieces of leftover black sugarpaste into sausage shapes and bending in the middle. Attach to the middle of each car, in front of the seat hole, using a dab of edible glue.

heads up...
If you're making scarves, place them round the necks before attaching the head.

for the drivers

1 Use the trimmings of the coloured sugarpastes to make the drivers. For each person, mould 20g (¾oz) sugarpaste into a sausage shape for the body. Feel for the hole in the top of the whoopie and push the body into it.

2 Roll thin sausages for arms and attach to the shoulders with a dab of edible glue. Flatten the ends slightly for the hands. Push a piece of dry spaghetti down through the body and into the whoopie, leaving 2cm (¾in) showing at the top to support the head.

3 For each head, roll 7g (¼oz) flesh-coloured sugarpaste into a ball. Pipe a dot of royal icing around the base of the spaghetti and push the head down onto the shoulders. Roll a tiny dot of sugarpaste into a ball for the nose and fix in place with a dab of edible glue.

4 Paint the facial features with edible dusts and pipe the hair with royal icing. Use the sugarpaste trimmings to add hats and scarves.

5 Pipe numbers on the front of each car and push half a stick of dry spaghetti into the back of each whoopie for the pole. Position the cars on the board, securing with a little royal icing.

make it special...
Paint the features and pipe the hair of the drivers to resemble the guests at your party.

Recipes   whoopies, buttercream, royal icing   *Techniques*   colouring, making figures, piping hair, painting faces

suppliers

UK

Almond Art
Units 15/16
Faraday Close
Gorse Lane Ind Est
Clacton On Sea
Essex CO15 4TR
Tel: 01255 223322
www.almondart.com

Lakeland
51 stores nationwide
Tel: 01539 488100
www.lakeland.co.uk

Squires Group
Squires House
3 Waverley Lane
Farnham
Surrey GU9 8BB
Tel: 0845 6171810
www.squires-shop.com

Waitrose
Stores nationwide
Tel: 0800 188 884
www.waitrose.com

US

Candyland Retail Store
201 W. Main Street
Somerville
NJ 08876
Tel: (908) 685 0410
www.candylandcrafts.com

New York Cake Supplies
56 W. 22nd Street
New York
NY 10010
Tel: (800) 942 2539
www.nycake.com

Wilton Industries
2240 W. 75th Street
Woodridge
IL 60517
Tel: (630) 963 1818
www.wilton.com

about the authors

Jill Collins and Natalie Saville co-own and run The Great Little Cake Company – a highly successful (and deliciously addictive) cake business, specializing in beautiful and creative wedding and celebration cakes. They have made cakes for a host of celebrities, have been featured on TV and have appeared regularly in various wedding magazines. This is their first book. For more information, contact details and a gallery of cake creations visit:
www.thegreatlittlecakecompany.co.uk

acknowledgments

We would like to thank everyone at David & Charles, especially Ali Myer, James Brooks and Sarah Clark for believing in us and supporting us throughout our first foray into the world of books. Also, our project editor Ame Verso for her brilliant editing, Sarah Underhill for the beautiful styling, and Sian Irvine and Joe Giacomet for the wonderful photographs.

index

loved this book?

Tell us what you think and download a free bonus project:

http://lovethisbook.bakeme.com

Bake Me I'm Yours...
Christmas

Various
ISBN-13: 978-1-4463-0060-2

Over 20 festive projects, recipes and ideas from top sugarcraft designers to help you have a truly tasty Christmas.

Bake Me I'm Yours...
Cupcake Celebration

Lindy Smith
ISBN-13: 978-0-7153-3770-7

Celebrate in style, with over 25 irresistible cupcake ideas. Add that special touch to every occasion following the beautiful designs and delicious recipes.

Bake Me I'm Yours
Cupcake Love

Zoe Clark
ISBN-13: 978-0-7153-3781-3

An indulgent collection of cupcake projects, recipes and ideas for every romantic occasion. Tempt loved ones with the 20 gorgeous designs.

Fun & Original
Birthday Cakes

Maisie Parrish
ISBN-13: 978-0-7153-3833-9

Be amused and amazed by this incredible collection of brilliant birthday cakes. Add a personal touch to your celebrations with over 30 unique characters, decorations and toppers.

All details correct at time of printing.